Crochet Pro

Over 15 Crochet Projects Perfect for the
Winter Months

Table of Contents

Thank you for downloading this book, "Crochet Projects for Winter: Over 15 Crochet Projects Perfect for the Winter Months".

Please feel free to share this book with your friends and family. Please also take the time to write a short review on Amazon to share your thoughts.

The Basics of Knitting

How to Cast On

In order to begin knitting, simply make a foundation round of stitches on your needle by the process of "casting on".
1. Firstly, do a slip knot by looping strands of yarn into a pretzel-like shape and leave a strand at the end that is at least 3x the width of the thing you're knitting (if your scarf is 8", you will require a twenty four inch tail). Simply slip the knitting needle through the pretzel shape and tug the ends of the yarn in order to tighten it
To begin knitting, you will need to create a foundation row of stitches on your needle by "casting on."
2. Wrap the end of the yarn over your left thumb and the working yarn (ball end) over the left forefinger. Utilize your different fingers to get yarn lengths in left palm. Supplement needle upward through the circle on the thumb.
3. Using the needle, discover the working yarn that is on your forefinger, and draw it through the circle on your thumb. Expel the thumb from the circle. Keeping the yarn finishes secured in palm, reposition thumb, and tighten the new fastening on the right-hand needle. Proceed using these steps until you've thrown on the obliged number of join.

Knit Stitch How-To

Hold the needle with cast-on stitches in your left hand. Then wrap the yarn you are using around your left second finger, and hold it in back of the left-hand needle.
1. Add the right needle from the front to the back into the 1st cast on stitch on the left needle and hence open up a space for a stitch.
2. Get the working yarn with the right needle.
3. Get the yarn through the opened stitch.
4. Push the cast-on stitch off the left needle while holding the middle finger against the 2nd cast-on stitch to make sure that it doesn't slip off. The stitch on the right needle is the brand new knit stitch. Proceed in knitting across the cast-on row. When you have gotten rid of the last stitch from the left needle (completing a row),

exchange the needles and return the needle with the stitching to your left.

How to Purl

The purl stitch varies from the knit stitch in two major ways: The working yarn is held in the front of the task rather than from the behind, and the needle is embedded from the behind to the front rather than from the front to the behind. So hold the needle with cast-on fastens in your left hand then wrap the working yarn (ball end) around your left forefinger, and hold it before the work.
1. Then using the right-hand needle, go once again to from the front into the first cast-on fasten on the left-hand needle, opening up a line.
2. Lay the working yarn over the needle from the front to the behind by moving the left forefinger in a descending fashion.
3. Push the working yarn from the front to the behind through cast-on stitch and slip the cast-on stitch off the left-hand needle while holding the center finger against the second cast-on line to guarantee it doesn't accidentally slip off. The line on the right needle is the recently framed purl stitch. It's switch side resembles a V.

How to Pick Up a Dropped Stitch

If you accidentally miss a stitch or drop it while you knit, do not worry, it is easy to fix your mistake with a crochet hook.
1. With the knit side facing you, place the crochet hook inside, from the front to behind and into the loop of the dropped stitch.
2. Use the hook to catch the first horizontal "ladder," and pull it through the loop to the front.
3. Then repeat until all the ladders have been pulled through the loop. Place the stitch back onto the left needle, with the right of the loop on the front of the needle.
To pick up a dropped stitch that occurred on a purl knit, simply turn your work around, and repeat the steps for a dropped knit stitch.

How to Join Yarn

To join a new ball of yarn as you knit, just pause your knitting with the old color while leaving a 6" strand and start using the new ball of yarn, but also remember to leave a long strand of yarn behind. The first stitch is going to be loose, so pull the yarn ends to secure it.

How to Cast Off

The following instructions aids in stopping the stitches from falling apart once they have been taken away from the needle.

1. Knit two stitches. Pull in the left needle into the first stitch, bring up the 1st stitch over the 2nd stitch and then altogether completely off the needle. Proceed knitting in this fashion until all the stitches have been cast off. Using a pair of scissors, cut the working yarn and leave a 6" strand behind then tug the tail through the last stitch to fasten it.
2. Using a yarn needle, connect all the ends of the yarn through the backs of multiple stitches, taking up the surface loops only.

An Introduction to Crocheting

There are a few basic crocheting techniques that you may need to get a hang of. So here is a basic breakdown of them for you.

Slip Knot

1. Firstly, you need to make a loop and then hook another loop through the original loop.
2. Next you need to tighten the loop gently and carefully slide the knot up to the hook.

Chain Stitch

1. Do the whole 'yarn over hook' and then draw the yarn through to create a brand new loop without tightening the previous one.
2. Repeat the step above to form as many chains as the instructions suggest. It is important that you don't count the slip knot as a stitch.

Slip Stitch

1. Insert the hook into the work (it is the second chain from the hook), do a 'yarn over hook' and draw the yarn through both the work and loop in one swift move.

2. In order to join a chain ring with a slip stitch, you must insert a hook into the first chain, then place the yarn over hook and next you should draw it through both the work and the yarn on hook in just a single move.

Single Crochet

1. Firstly, you need to insert the hook into the work (this is the second chain from the hook on the starting chain), *yarn over hook and draw yarn only through the work.
2. Place the yarn over the hook again and then carefully draw the yarn through both the loops.
3. Now one single crochet has been made. Insert the hook into the following stitch: now repeat from * in step one.

Half Double Crochet

1. Firstly, place the yarn over the hook and insert it into the work (it is the third chain from the hook on the starting chain).
2. *Yarn over hook and draw through the work only.

3. Then place the yarn over the hook again and draw through all three loops.
4. Now that one half double crochet made, you should place the yarn over the hook again and insert it into the next stitch, then repeat from step two.

Double Crochet

1. Place the yarn over the hook and insert the hook into the work (this is the fourth chain from the hook on the starting chain).
2. Place the yarn over hook and draw through the work only.
3. Then place the yarn over the hook and draw through the first two loops on the hook only.
4. Next, place the yarn over hook and draw through the last two loops.
5. Now one double crochet has been created. So to repeat this process; place the yarn over the hook then insert it into the following stitch and repeat from step two.

Triple Crochet

1. Yarn over hook twice, then insert hook into next stitch.
2. Yarn over hook and draw yarn through stitch - (there are four loop on the hook)
3. Loop yarn over hook and draw through two loops, (there are now three loops remaining on the hook).
4. Yarn over hook and draw through two loops.
5. Again, loop yarn over hook and draw through the last two loops on the hook (there is now one loop remaining.)
This completes one treble crochet.

Cluster

Yarn over, insert hook in indicated stitch and draw up a loop, yarn over and draw through two loops on hook; [yarn over, insert hook in same stitch and draw up a loop, yarn over and draw through two loops on hook] three times; yarn over and draw through all five loops on hook.

Now that you have a basic understanding of both the crocheting and the knitting techniques, we can get started!

Winter Dog Outfit (Crochet)

MATERIALS:

- One Color of Yarn (1 Ball for S & M, 2 Balls for L & XL)
- Crochet Hook (Size 5mm)
- Marker

SIZES :

To fit the dog chest measurement: S (M-L-XL) 10 (13-16-24) inches.

INSTRUCTIONS:

These instructions are written for the smallest size. If you require changes in size, the extra instructions will be written in ( ).

Chain thirty four (38-48-64) loosely.

First Round (Right Side): One single crochet in the second chain from the hook. Do one single crochet in each chain across. Thirty three (37-47- 63) stitches. Turn.

Second Round: Chain one. Do one single crochet in each single crochet to the end of the round. Turn.

Proceed in the pattern as follows

First Round (Right Side): Chain one. Do one single crochet in the first stitch. * one double crochet in the next stitch. Add another single crochet in the next stitch. Now, repeat form * to the end of the round. Turn.

Second Round: Chain three (counts as double crochet). * one single crochet in the next double crochet. Then complete one double crochet in the next single crochet. Now, repeat from * to the end of the round. Turn.

Third Round: Chain one. Two single crochet in the first double crochet (an increase is made). * one double crochet in the next single crochet. Do one single crochet in the next double crochet. Repeat from * to the last two stitches. Then add another double crochet in the next single crochet. Two single crochet in the last double crochet (an increase is made). Turn.

Fourth Round: Chain three (counts as double crochet). Now, do one double crochet in the first single crochet (an increase is made) * one double crochet in the next single crochet. Add another single crochet in the next double crochet. Repeat from * to the last two stitches. Then complete one double crochet in the next single crochet. Two double crochet in the last single crochet (an increase is made0. Turn.

Fifth Round: Chain one. Two single crochet in the first double crochet (an increase is made). Now, complete one double crochet in the next double crochet. * one single crochet in the next double crochet. Do double crochet in the next single crochet. Repeat from * to the last three stitches. Do one single crochet in the next double crochet. Now do double crochet in the next double crochet. Two single crochet in the last double crochet (an increase is made). Turn. Repeat the fourth and fifth rounds 0 (1-2-4) time(s) more, then repeat the fourth round 0 (1-0-1) more time. 39 (49-61-87) stitches.   Work 1 (0-1-0) round even in pattern.

Leg Openings

First Round (Right Side): Pattern across 3 (5-7-9) stitches. Slip stitch across the next 5 (5-5-7) stitches. Chain one. Pattern across 23 (29- 37-55) stitches. Slip stitch across the next 5 (5-5-7) stitches. Continue the pattern until the end of row.

Note: All parts of the leg sections are worked simultaneously using different balls of yarn for every section.

Work 1 (11/2-11/2-21/2) inches in pattern, ending with a right side row.

Joining (Wrong Side):

The pattern across will be 3 (5-7- 9) stitches. Chain 5 (5-5-7). Pattern across 23 (29-37-55) stitches. Chain 5 (5-5-7). Pat to the end of the row.

First Round: Pattern across 3 (5-7-9) stitches. Pattern across the next 5 (5-5-7) chain. Pattern across 23 (29-37-55) stitches. Pattern across the next 5 (5-5- 7) chains. Pattern to the end of the row. 39 (49-61- 87) stitches.

Continue going on with an even pattern until the work after the neckband measures 5 (61/2-8-11) inches, finally ending with a wrong side row. Place the marker at the end of each last row.

Back Shaping

First Round: Slip stitch across the first 4 (5-6-9) stitches. Chain one. Pattern to the last 4 (5- 6-9) stitches. Turn. Leave remaining stitches unworked. 31 (39-49-69) stitches.

Second Round: Chain one. Draw up a loop in each of the first two stitches. Yarn over hook and draw through all the loops on the hook – single crochet two stitches together made. Pattern to the last two stitches. Single crochet two stitches together over the last two stitches. Turn.

Repeat the last round 5 (5-8-9) more times. 19 (27-31-49) stitches remaining. Continue an even pattern until the work after the neckband measures 10 (121/2-151/2- 21) inches, ending with a wrong side row. Fasten off.

Back Edging

First Round (Right Side): Join the yarn with a slip stitch at the marker. Chain one. Work single crochet evenly across the back edge until the opposite marker. Turn.

Second Round: Chain one. Do one single crochet in each single crochet across. Fasten off.

Now sew the neck and the belly seam.

Leg Edging

First Round (Right Side): Join the yarn with a slip stitch at the leg opening. Chain one. Now work single crochet evenly around. Join with a slip stitch to the first single crochet.

Second Round: Chain one. One single crochet in each of the single crochet around. Join with a slip stitch to the first single crochet. Fasten off.

Winter Baby Shoes (Knit)

MEASUREMENTS:

Fits three-six months (twelve-eighteen months)

MATERIALS:

- Red Yarn (one Ball)
- Two Buttons
- Size 3.25 mm Knitting Needles
- Thread and Needle

INSTRUCTIONS:

These instructions are written for the smallest size. If there are changes that need to be made for the larger sizes, the instructions will be written in the ( ).

Cast on 45 (55) stitches.

First Round (Wrong Side): Knit.

Second Round: Increase one stitch in the first stitch. Knit 21 (26). Make two stitches. Knit 20 (25). Increase a stitch in the next stitch. Knit one stitch. 49 (59) stitches.

Third and Alt Rounds: Knit.

Fourth Round: Increase one stitch in the first stitch. Knit 23 (28). Make two stitches. Knit 22 (27). Increase one stitch in the next stitch. Knit one stitch. 53 (63) stitches.

Sixth Rounds: Increase one stitch in the first stitch. Knit 25 (30). Make two. Knit 24 (29). Increase one stitch in the next stitch. Knit one stitch. 57 (67) stitches.

Eighth Round: Increase one stitch in the first stitch. Knit 27 (32). Make two stitches. Knit 26 (31). Increase one stitch in the next stitch. Knit one stitch. 61 (71) stitches.

Ninth Round: Knit.

Size 12-18 Months Only

Tenth Round: Increase one stitch in the first stitch. Knit thirty four stitches. Make two stitches. Knit thirty three stitches. Increase one stitch in the next stitch. Knit one stitch. Seventy five stitches.

Eleventh Round: Knit.

Both Sizes

Work the next eight rounds using the stocking stitch and end with the right side facing for the next round.

Shape Instep

First Round (Right Side): Knit 35 (43). Slip one knit. Turn. Leave the remaining stitches onto the spare needle.

Second Round: Purl two stitches together through back loops. Purl 7 (9). Purl two stitches together. Slip one purl. Turn.

Third Round: Knit the next two stitches together. Knit 7 (9). Slip the next stitch. Knit one stitch. Pass slip stitch over. Slip one knit. Turn.

Repeat the last two rounds one (two) more time(s).

Next Round: Same as the second round.

Next Round: Knit the next two stitches together. Knit 7 (9). Slip the next stitch. Knit one stitch. Pass the slip stitch over. Knit to the end of the row. Work two rounds garter stitch (knit every round) across all the stitches. Cast off knit ways (Wrong Side). Sew the back and the sole seam.

Strap

Cast on five stitches and note that the first round is wrong side, work 11/2 inches in garter stitches ending with the right side facing for the next round.

Next Round: Knit two. Yarn over. Knit the next two stitches together (buttonhole). Knit one stitch. Knit three rounds even.

Next Round: Knit the next two stitches together. Knit one stitch. Knit the next two stitches together. Three stitches.

Next Round: Knit three stitches.

Next Round: Slip next knit. Knit the next two stitches together. Pass slip stitch over. Fasten off. Then using a thread and a needle, sew the strap in position. Finally, sew the button to correspond to the buttonhole.

Winter Baby Pom Pom Hat (Crochet)

MEASUREMENTS:

To fit baby's head 3/6 (6/12-18/24) mos.

MATERIALS:

- Yarn (One - Two Balls)
- Crochet Hook (8 mm)
- Thread and Needle
- Scissors

INSTRUCTIONS:

These instructions are written for the smallest size. If there are changes that need to be made for the larger sizes, the instructions will be written in the ( ).

Chain 47 (56-61).

First Round: One single crochet in the second chain from the hook.

Now complete one single crochet in each chain to the end of the chain. Turn. 46 (55-60) single crochet.

Second Round: Chain one. Then complete one single crochet in each single crochet to the end of the round. Turn.

Third Round: Chain one. (One single crochet. Two double crochet) in the first single crochet. * Skip the next two single crochet. (One single crochet. Two double crochet) in the next single crochet). Repeat form * to the last three single crochet. Skip the next two single crochet. Then complete one single crochet in the last single crochet. Turn.

Fourth Round: Chain one. (One single crochet. Two double crochet) in the first single crochet. * Skip the next two double crochet. (One single crochet. Two double crochet) in the next double crochet. Now, repeat from * to the last single crochet in the last single crochet. Turn.

Repeat the last round for the pattern until the work from the beginning measures 6 (7-8)" [15 (18-20.5) cm]. Fasten off. Fold the piece in half. Using a thread and needle, sew the side and the top seam together.

Pompom (make 2)

Twirl the yarn around three of your fingers approximately fifty times. Then remove the yarn from your fingers and tie them tightly in the center. Cut through each side of the loops. Trim to a smooth, round shape. Using the thread and needle, sew one pompom to each top corner of the hat.

Winter Gingham Blanket (Crochet)

MATERIALS:

- Two Different Colors of Yarn (2 Balls Each)
- Crochet Hook (5.5 mm)

INSTRUCTIONS:

Note: The entire blanket is worked holding two strands of yarn together.

When changing colors, work to last two loops on the hook of the last double crochet. Then draw the new color through the last two loops to complete the stitch and proceed in the new color.

Work over the unused color in the gingham pattern then carry the colors up the side of work.

Strip One (make three)

With two strand of the MAIN COLOR, chain three.

First Round: One double crochet in the fourth chain from the hook (counts as two double crochet). One double crochet in the next chain. * Using COLOR A, one double crochet in each of the next three chains. Then using the MAIN COLOR, one double crochet in each of the next three chains. Repeat from * to the end of the chain. Turn. Twenty one double crochet.

Second Round: Using the MAIN COLOR, chain three (counts as double crochet.) One double crochet in each of the next two double crochet. * Using COLOR A, one double crochet in each of the next three double crochet. Then using the MAIN COLOR, one double crochet in each of the next three double crochet. Repeat from * to the end of the row. Join B. Turn.

Third Round: Using COLOR B, chain three (counts as double crochet). One double crochet in each of the next two double crochet. * With the MAIN COLOR, one double crochet in each of the next three double crochet. Then using COLOR B, one double crochet in each of the next three double crochet. Repeat from * to the end of the row. Turn.

Fourth Round: Repeat the third round. Join the MAIN COLOR.

Fifth Round: Using the MAIN COLOR, chain three (counts as double crochet). One double crochet in each of the next two double crochet. * Using COLOR A, one double crochet in each of the next three double crochet. Then using the MAIN COLOR, one double crochet in each of the next three double crochet. Repeat from * to the end of the round. Turn.

Sixth Round: Repeat the second round. Repeat the last four rounds of the pattern twelve more times. Fasten off.

Strip Two (make one)

Using two strand of the MAIN COLOR, chain twenty three.

First Round: One double crochet in the fourth chain from the hook (counts as two double crochet). One double crochet in each chain to the end of the chain. Turn. Twenty one double crochet.

Second Round: Chain three (counts as a double crochet). One double crochet in each double crochet to the end of the round. Join COLOR B. Turn.

Third and Fourth Rounds: Using COLOR B, repeat the second round. Join the MAIN COLOR at the end of the fourth round.

Fifth and Sixth Rounds: Using the MAIN COLOR, repeat the second round. Repeat the third to sixth rounds of the stripe pattern until fifty four rounds have been worked. Fasten off.

FINISHING

Sew the strips together, as follows: one, two, one, two, one.

Edging

Join two strand of the MAIN COLOR with a slip stitch in the top right hand corner. Chain one. Three single crochet in the same space as the slip stitch. Work in single crochet evenly around the blanket, having three single crochet in each corner. Join with a slip stitch to the first single crochet. Fasten off.

Winter Shawl (Knit)

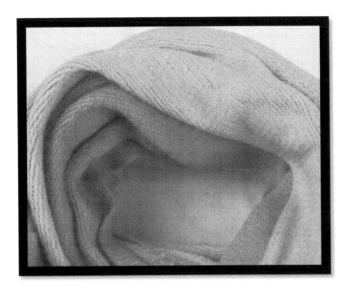

MATERIALS:

- Knitting Needle (5 mm)
- Circular Knitting Needle (5 mm)
- Two Different Colors of Yarn (2 Balls of Each)
- Marker

INSTRUCTIONS:

Note: Switch to the circular knitting needle when necessary to accommodate all the different stitches.

Using COLOR A, cast on three stitches.

First Round (Wrong Side): Increase one stitch by knitting into the front and back of the next stitch. Knit one stitch. Increase one stitch by knitting into the front and back of the next stitch. Five stitches.

Second Round: Increase one stitch by knitting into the front and back of the next stitch. Knit to the last stitch. Increase one stitch by knitting into the front and back of the next stitch. Repeat the last round until there are nineteen stitches. Do not break COLOR A and join COLOR B.

Next Round (Right Side): Using COLOR B, repeat the second round. Twenty one stitches.

Next Round: Increase one stitch by knitting into the front and back of the next stitch. Knit to the last three stitches. Turn. Leave the remaining stitches unworked.

Next Round: Slip the next stitch. Now, place the marker on the last worked stitch. Knit to the last stitch. Increase one stitch by knitting into the front and back of the next stitch.

Next Round: Increase one stitch by knitting into the front and back of the next stitch. Knit to three stitches before the marked stitch. Turn. Leave the remaining stitches on a spare needle. Repeat the last two rounds ten more times.

Next Round: Slip the next stitch. Knit to the last stitch. Increase one stitch by knitting into the front and back of the next stitch.

Next Round: Increase one stitch by knitting into the front and back of the next stitch. Knit across all the stitches to the last stitch. Increase one stitch by knitting into the front and back of the next stitch. Forty seven stitches. Break COLOR B.

Next Round: Using COLOR A, increase one stitch by knitting into the front and back of the next stitch. Knit to the last five stitches. Turn. Leave the remaining stitches on a spare needle.

Next Round: Slip the next stitch. Then place marker on the last worked stitch. Knit to the last stitch. Increase one stitch by knitting into the front and back of the next stitch.

Next Round: Increase one stitch by knitting into the front and back of the next stitch. Knit to four stitches before the marked stitch. Turn. Leave the remaining stitches on a spare needle. Repeat the last two round ten more times.

Next Round: Slip the next stitch. Knit to the last stitch. Increase one stitch by knitting into the front and back of the next stitch. Do not break COLOR A and join COLOR B. Seventy one stitches.

Next Round (Right Side): Using COLOR B, increase one stitch by knitting into the front and back of the next stitch. Knit across all the stitches to the last stitch. Increase one stitch by knitting into the front and back of the next stitch. Seventy three stitches.

Next Round: Increase one stitch by knitting into the front and back of the next stitch. Knit to the last seven stitches. Turn. Leave the remaining stitches on a spare needle.

Next Round: Slip the next stitch. Then place the marker on the last worked stitch. Knit to the last stitch. Increase one stitch by knitting into the front and back of the next stitch.

Next Round: Increase one stitch by knitting into the front and back of the next stitch. Knit to the six stitches before the marked stitches. Turn. Leave the remaining stitches on a spare needle. Repeat the last two rounds ten more times.

Next Round: Slip the next stitch. Knit to the last stitch. Increase one stitch by knitting into the front and back of the next stitch.

Next Round: Increase one stitch by knitting into the front and back of the next stitch. Knit across all the stitches to the last stitch. Increase one stitch by knitting into the front and back of the next stitch. Ninety nine stitches. Break COLOR B.

Winter Set - Scarf, Hat, Mitts (Knit)

MEASUREMENTS:

Mittens and Hat: One size to fit average lady. Scarf: Approximately 7 x 70 inches [18 x 178 cm].

MATERIALS:

- Cable Needle
- Set of four size 6.5 mm (U.S. 101/2) double-pointed knitting needles.
- Size 8 mm (U.S. 11) knitting needles or size needed to obtain gauge.
- Mittens Hat Scarf - 3 ball(s)
- Needle and Thread
- Scissors
- Safety Pin

INSTRUCTIONS:

Scarf

Cast on twenty eight stitches.

First Round (Right Side): Knit one stitch. * Slip the next stitch onto the cable needle and hold it at the back of the work, knit the next stitch from the left hand needle then knit stitch from the cable needle. Knit two stitches. Repeat from * to the last three stitches. Slip the next stitch onto the cable needle and hold it at the back of the work, knit the next stitch from the left hand needle then knit stitch from the cable needle. Knit one stitch.

Second Round: Knit one stitch. * Purl two stitches. Knit two stitches. Repeat from * to the last three stitches. Purl two stitches. Knit one stitch. Repeat the last two rounds for pattern until the scarf measures 70 inches [178 centimeters], ending with a wrong side row. Cast off.

Hat

Cast on sixty four stitches.

First Round (Right Side): Knit one stitch. * Slip the next stitch onto the cable needle and hold it at the back of the work, knit the next stitch from the left hand needle then knit stitch from the cable needle. Knit two stitches. Repeat from * to the last three stitches. Slip the next stitch onto the cable needle and hold it at the back of the work, knit the next stitch from the left hand needle then knit stitch from the cable needle. Knit one stitch.

Second Round: Knit one stitch. * Purl two stitches. Knit two stitches. Repeat from * to the last three stitches. Purl two stitches. Knit one stitch. Repeat the last two rounds for pattern until the work from the beginning measures three inches [7.5 centimeters], ending with a second round.

Note: At this point, the wrong side becomes the right side and the right side becomes the wrong side for cuff turnback.

Next Round: Repeat the second round.

Next Round: Repeat the first round.

Repeat the last two rounds for pattern until the work from the beginning measures eight inches [20.5 centimeters], ending with a wrong side row.

Shape Top

First Round (Right Side): Knit one stitch. * Slip the next stitch onto the cable needle and hold it at the back of the work, knit the next stitch from the left hand needle then knit stitch from the cable needle. Knit two stitches. Slip the next stitch onto the cable needle and hold it at the back of the work, knit the next stitch from the left hand needle then knit stitch from the cable needle. Knit the next two stitches together. Repeat from * to the last seven stitches. Slip the next stitch onto the cable needle and hold it at the back of the work, knit the next stitch from the left hand needle then knit stitch from the cable needle. Knit two stitches. Slip the next stitch onto the cable needle and hold it at the back of the work, knit the next stitch from the left hand needle then knit stitch from the cable needle. Knit one stitch. Fifty seven stitches.

Second Round: Knit one stitch. Purl two stitches. *Knit two stitches. Purl two stitches. Knit one stitch. Purl two stitches. Repeat from * to the last five stitches. Knit two stitches. Purl two stitches. Knit one stitch.

Third Round: Knit one stitch. * Slip the next stitch onto the cable needle and hold it at the back of the work, knit the next stitch from the left hand needle then knit stitch from the cable needle. Knit the next two stitches together. Slip the next stitch onto the cable needle and hold it at the back of the work, knit the next stitch from the left hand needle then knit stitch from the cable needle. Knit one stitch. Repeat from * to the last seven stitches. Slip the next stitch onto the cable needle and hold it at the back of the work, knit the next stitch from the left hand needle then knit stitch from the cable needle. Knit the next two stitches together. Slip the next stitch onto the cable needle and hold it at the back of the work, knit the next stitch from the left hand needle then knit stitch from the cable needle. Knit one stitch. Forty nine stitches.

Fourth Round: Knit one stitch. *Purl two stitches. Knit one stitch. Repeat from * to the last three stitches. Purl two stitches. Knit one stitch.

Fifth Round: Knit one stitch. * (Slip the next stitch onto the cable needle and hold it at the back of the work, knit the next stitch from the left hand needle then knit stitch from the cable needle. Knit one stitch) twice. Knit the next two stitches together. Knit one stitch. Repeat from * to the last three stitches. Slip the next stitch onto the cable needle and hold it at the back of the work, knit the next stitch from the left hand needle then knit stitch from the cable needle. Knit one stitch. Forty four stitches.

Sixth Round: Knit one stitch. Purl two stitches. Knit three stitches. *(Purl two stitches. Knit one stitch) twice. Knit two stitches. Repeat from * to the last six stitches. (Purl two stitches. Knit one stitch) twice.

Seventh Round: Knit one stitch. * Slip the next stitch onto the cable needle and hold it at the back of the work, knit the next stitch from the left hand needle then knit stitch from the cable needle. Knit one stitch. Knit the next two stitches together. Knit three stitches. Repeat from * to the last three stitches. Slip the next stitch onto the cable needle and hold it at the back of the work, knit the next stitch from the left hand needle then knit stitch from the cable needle. Knit one stitch. Thirty nine stitches.

Eighth Round: Knit one stitch. *Purl two stitches. Knit five stitches. Repeat from * to the last three stitches. Purl two stitches. Knit one stitch.

Ninth Round: Knit one stitch. * Slip the next stitch onto the cable needle and hold it at the back of the work, knit the next stitch from the left hand needle then knit stitch from the cable needle. Knit one stitch. Knit the next two stitches together. Knit two stitches. Repeat from * to the last three stitches. Slip the next stitch onto the cable needle and hold it at the back of the work, knit the next stitch from the left hand needle then knit stitch from the cable needle. Knit one stitch. Thirty four stitches.

Tenth Round: Knit one stitch. * Purl two stitches. Knit the next two stitches together. Knit two stitches. Repeat from * to the last three stitches. Purl two stitches. Knit one stitch. Twenty nine stitches.

Eleventh Round: Knit one stitch. * Slip the next stitch onto the cable needle and hold it at the back of the work, knit the next stitch from the left hand needle then knit stitch from the cable needle. Knit the next two stitches together. Knit one stitch. Repeat from * to the last three stitches. Slip the next stitch onto the cable needle and hold it at the back of the work, knit the next stitch from the left hand needle then knit stitch from the cable needle. Knit one stitch. Twenty four stitches.

Twelfth Round: Knit one stitch. *Purl two stitches. Knit the next two stitches together. Repeat from * to the last three stitches. Purl two stitches. Knit one stitch. Nineteen stitches.

Thirteenth Round: Knit one stitch. *Knit one stitch. Knit the next two stitches together. Repeat from * to the end of the round. Thirteen stitches.

Break the yarn, leaving a long end. Thread the end through the remaining stitches and tighten securely, Then using a thread and needle, sew back the seam, reversing the bottom three inches [7.5 cm] for turn back.

Mittens (Right and Left make alike)

Using a set of four double-pointed needles, cast on twenty four stitches. Divide the stitches on three needles. Join in round. Mark the first stitch with a contrasting thread.

Firs Round: *Knit two stitches. Purl two stitches. Repeat from * around. Repeat the last round of (Knit two stitches. Purl two stitches) ribbing for two inches [five centimeters], increasing by four stitches evenly across the last round. Twenty eight stitches.

Continue in pattern as follows:

First Round: * Slip the next stitch onto the cable needle and hold it at the back of the work, knit the next stitch from the left hand needle then knit stitch from the cable needle. Knit two stitches. Repeat from * around.

Second Round: *Knit two stitches. Purl two stitches. Repeat from * around. Repeat the last two rounds of the pattern two more times.

Shape Thumb Gusset

First Round: Pattern fourteen stitches. Make one stitch by picking up the horizontal loop lying before the next stitch and knitting it into the back of the loop. Continue pattern till the end of the round.

Second Round: Pattern fourteen stitches. Purl one stitch. Continue pattern to the end of the round.

Third Round: Pattern fourteen stitches. Make one stitch by picking up the horizontal loop lying before the next stitch and knitting it into the back of the loop. Knit one stitch. Make one stitch by picking up the horizontal loop lying before the next stitch and knitting it into the back of the loop. Continue pattern to the end of the round.

Fourth Round: Pattern fourteen stitches. Purl three stitches. Continue pattern to the end of the round.

Fifth Round: Pattern fourteen stitches. Make one stitch by picking up the horizontal loop lying before the next stitch and knitting it into the back of the loop. Knit three stitches. Make one stitch by picking up the horizontal loop lying before the next stitch and knitting it into the back of the loop. Continue pattern to the end of the round.

Sixth Round: Pattern fourteen stitches. Purl five stitches. Continue pattern to the end of the round.

Seventh Round: Pattern fourteen stitches. Make one stitch by picking up the horizontal loop lying before the next stitch and knitting it into the back of the loop. Knit five stitches. Make one stitch by picking up the horizontal loop lying before the next stitch and knitting it into the back of the loop. Continue pattern to the end of the round.

Eighth Round: Pattern fourteen stitches. Purl seven stitches. Continue pattern to the end of the round.

Ninth Round: Pattern fourteen stitches. Slip the next seven stitches onto a safety pin (thumb opening). Continue pattern to the end of the round. Twenty eight stitches. Pattern in rounds until the work from the beginning measures 8 1/2 inches [21.5 centimeters], ending with a second round of pattern.

Shape Top

First Round: * Slip the next stitch onto the cable needle and hold it at the back of the work, knit the next stitch from the left hand needle then knit stitch from the cable needle. Knit the next two stitches together. Repeat from * around. Eighteen stitches remaining.
Second Round: *Knit one stitch. Purl two stitches together. Repeat from * around. Twelve stitches remaining.

Third Round: *Purl two stitches together. Repeat form * around. Six stitches remaining.

Then break the yarn and leave behind a long end. Thread the end through the remaining stitches and tighten securely.

Thumb

Knit seven stitches from safety pin. Pick up and knit one stitch at the base of the thumb. Divide these eight stitches onto three needles.

Next Round: Purl.

Next Round: Knit.

Repeat the last two rounds until the work from the pick up round measures two inches [five centimeters], ending with a purl round.

Next Round: Four times. Four stitches remain. Break the yarn and leave a long end. Thread the end through the remaining stitches and tighten securely.

Winter Baby Cap (Crochet)

MATERIALS:

- One Color of Yarn (One Ball)
- Crochet Hook (3.75 mm)

INSTRUCTIONS:

These instructions are written for smallest size.

Note: Chain three at the beginning of the round counts as double crochet.

Chain four.

First Round: Eleven double crochet in the fourth chain from the hook. Join with a slip stitch to the top of chain three. Twelve double crochet.

Second Round: Chain three. One double crochet in the same space as the last slip stitch. * two double crochet in the next double crochet. Now, repeat from * around. Join with a slip stitch to the top of chain three. Twenty four double crochet.

Third Round: Chain three. * two double crochet in the next double crochet. Now you should do one double crochet in the next double crochet. Then now repeat from * to the last double crochet. Two double crochet in the last double crochet. Join with a slip stitch to the top of chain three. Thirty six double crochet.

Fourth Round: Chain three. * two double crochet in the next double crochet. Add one double crochet in each of the next two double crochet. Repeat from * to the last two double crochet. Two double crochet in the next double crochet. Now, add another one double crochet in the last double crochet. Join with a slip stitch to the top of chain three. Forty eight double crochet.

Fifth Round: Chain three. * two double crochet in the next double crochet. Now, you should do one double crochet in each of the next eleven (three - two) double crochet. Repeat from * to the last eleven (three - two) double crochet. Two double crochet in the next double crochet. Now add another double crochet in each of the last ten (two-one) double crochet. Join with a slip stitch to the top of chain three. Fifty two (sixty – sixty four) double crochet.

Sixth Round: Chain three. Now you should do one double crochet in each double crochet around. Join with a slip stitch to the top of chain three. Repeat the last round until the work from the beginning measures 31/2 (41/2-41/2) inches.

Size Eighteen Months Only

First Round: Chain three. * one double crochet in each of the next fourteen double crochet. (Yarn over hook and draw up a loop in the next double crochet. Yarn over hook and draw through two loops on hook) twice. Yarn over hook and draw through all loops on the hook – double crochet two stitches together made. Now, repeat from * three more times. Join with a slip stitch to the top of chain three. Sixty double crochet.

All Sizes

Edging

First Round: Chain one. One single crochet in the same space as the last slip stitch. * Chain five. Miss the next three double crochets. Do one single crochet in the next double crochet. Repeat from * around, omitting single crochet at the end of the last repeat. Join with a slip stitch to the first single crochet.

Second Round: Chain five. * one single crochet in the next five space chain. Chain two. (Yarn over hook and draw up a loop. Yarn over hook and draw through two loops on the hook) three times in the next single crochet. Yarn over hook and draw through all loops on the hook – creating a cluster. Chain two. One single crochet in the next five space chain. Chain five. Repeat from * across, ending with chain two. Slip stitch in the third chain of chain five.

Third Round: Chain one. One single crochet in the same space as the last slip stitch. * Chain five. Now add one single crochet in the next cluster. Chain five. One single crochet in the next five space chain. Repeat from * around, ending with chain five. Join with a slip stitch to the first single crochet. Fasten off.

Winter Baby Blanket (Crochet)

MEASUREMENTS:

Approximately 35" x 39" [89 x 99 cm].

MATERIALS:

- Yarn (4 Balls)
- Crochet Hook (5 mm)

INSTRUCTIONS:

Chain one hundred and five.

First Round (Right Side): One double crochet in the fourth chain from the hook (counts as two double crochet). Two double crochet in each of the next two chains. (Skip the next chain. Then do one double crochet in the next chain) five times. * Skip the next chain. Two double crochet in each of the next six chains. (Skip the next chain. Next, do one double crochet in the next chain) five times.

Then repeat from * to the last four chains. Skip the next chain. Two double crochet in each of the last three chains. Turn.

Second Round: Chain one. One single crochet in each double crochet across. Turn.

Third Round: Chain three (counts as double crochet). Then do one double crochet in the first single crochet. Two double crochet in each of the next two single crochet. (Skip the next single crochet. One double crochet in the next single crochet) five times. * Skip the next single crochet. Two double crochet in each of next six single crochet. (Skip the next single crochet. One double crochet in the next single crochet) five times. Repeat from * to the last four single crochet. Skip the next single crochet. Two double crochet in each of the last three single crochet. Turn. Repeat the last two rounds until the blanket measures approximately thirty nine inches. Fasten off.

Side Edging

With the right side facing up, join with a slip stitch to the bottom right hand corner. Chain one. Work one row of single crochet evenly along the side edge. Fasten off.

Repeat for the other side.

Winter Beret (Crochet)

MATERIALS:

- One Color of Yarn (1 Ball)
- Crochet Hook (Size 5mm)

INSTRUCTIONS:

Chain six. Join with a slip stitch to the first chain to form a ring.

First Round: Chain one. Twelve single crochet in ring. Join with a slip stitch to the first single crochet.

Second Round: Chain one. (One single crochet in the next single crochet. Two single crochet in the next single crochet) six times. Join with a slip stitch to the first single crochet. Eighteen single crochet.

Third Round: Chain one. (One single crochet in each of the next two single crochet. Two single crochet in the next single crochet) six times. Join with a slip stitch to the first single crochet. Twenty four single crochet.

Fourth Round: Chain one. (One single crochet in each of the next three single crochet. Two single crochet in the next single crochet) six times. Join with a slip stitch to the first single crochet. Thirty single crochet.

Fifth Round: Chain one. (One single crochet in each of the next four single crochet. Two single crochet in the next single crochet) six times. Join with a slip stitch to the first single crochet. Thirty six single crochet. Continue in the same manner, include six stitches in each round, as established to one hundred and twenty single crochet.

Sixth to Seventh Rounds: Chain one. Do one single crochet in each of the single crochets around. Join with a slip stitch to the first single crochet at the end of the second round.

Eighth Round: Chain one. Do one single crochet in each of the first eighteen single crochet. Draw up a loop in each of the next two single crochet. Yarn over hook and draw through all loops on the hook –single crochet two stitches together made. * One single crochet in each of the next eighteen single crochet. Single crochet two stitches together. Then repeat from * four more times. Join with a slip stitch to the first single crochet. One hundred and fourteen stitches.

Ninth Round: Chain one. * One single crochet in each of the next seventeen stitches. Single crochet two stitches together. Then repeat from * five more times. Join with a slip stitch to the first single crochet. One hundred and eight stitches.

Tenth Round: Chain one. * one single crochet in each of the next seven stitches. Single crochet two stitches together. Now repeat from * eleven more times. Join with a slip stitch to the first single crochet. Ninety six stitches.

Twelfth Round: Chain one. * one single crochet in each of the next ten stitches. Single crochet two stitches together. Now repeat from * seven more times. Join with a slip stitch to the first single crochet. Eighty eight stitches.

Thirteenth Round: Chain one. * one single crochet in each of the next nine stitches. Single crochet two stitches together. Then repeat from * seven more times. Join with a slip stitch to the first single crochet. Eighty stitches.

Fourteenth Round: Chain one. * one single crochet in each of the next six stitches. Single crochet two stitches together. Now repeat from * nine more times. Join with a slip stitch to the first single crochet. Seventy stitches.

Fifteenth Round: Chain one. * One single crochet in each of the next five stitches. Single crochet two stitches together. Then repeat from * nine more times. Join with a slip stitch to the first single crochet. Sixty stitches.

Sixteenth Round: Chain one. * one single crochet in each of the next eight stitches. Single crochet two stitches together. Then repeat from * five more times. Join with a slip stitch to the first single crochet. Fifty four stitches.

Seventeenth to Nineteenth Round: Chain one. Do one single crochet in each stitch around. Join with a slip stitch to the first single crochet. Fasten off.

Winter Mittens (Crochet)

MATERIALS:

- Two Different Colored Yarn (One Ball of Each)
- Crochet Hook (Size 5 mm)
- Ribbon

INSTRUCTIONS:

NOTES

The mittens are worked from the stripped cuff upwards. These are worked back and forth in rows then seamed together.

To change the color, you need to work the last stitch of the old color to the last yarn over. Then you should yarn over with the other color and draw through all the loops on the hook in order to complete the stitch. Don't try and fasten off the old color. Carry colors not in use across to the wrong side of the mitten until it is needed.

MITTEN (Make Two)

With COLOR A, chain twenty one.

Round One (Right Side): Single crochet in the second chain from the hook and in each of the remaining chains across, tur – twenty single crochet.

Round Two: Chain one. Single crochet in each single crochet across, turn; switch to COLOR B in the last single crochet.

Round Three and Four: With COLOR B, chain one, single crochet in each single crochet across, turn. Then COLOR B chain one, two single crochet in the first single crochet, single crochet in each of the single crochet across, two single crochet in the last single crochet, turn – twenty two single crochet.

THUMB SHAPE

Round Five: Chain one, single crochet in the first ten single crochet, two single crochet in the next two single crochet, single crochet in the last ten single crochet, turn – twenty four single crochet.

Round Six: Chain one, single crochet in the first ten single crochet, two single crochet in the next single crochet, single crochet in the next two single crochet, two single crochet in the next single crochet, single crochet in the last ten single crochet, turn – twenty six single crochet.

Round Seven: Chain one, single crochet in the first ten single crochet, two single crochet in the next single crochet, single crochet in the next four single crochet, two single crochet in the next single crochet, single crochet in the last ten single crochet, turn – twenty eight single crochet.

DIVIDE FOR HAND AND THUMB

Round Eight: Chain one, single crochet in the first ten single crochet, skip the next eight single crochet (for thumb), single crochet in the next ten single crochet, turn – twenty single crochet.

Round Nine: Chain one, single crochet in each single crochet across, turn. Repeat the last round until the hand measures four and a half inches, measured for the last COLOR C row.

TOP OF HAND

Round Ten: Chain one, single crochet two stitches together, single crochet in the next single crochet; repeat from * across to the last two single crochet, single crochet two stitches together, turn – thirteen single crochet.

Round Eleven: Chain one, *single crochet two stitches together; repeat from * across to the last stitch, single crochet in the last stich, turn – seven single crochet.

Fasten off and leave a long strand for gathering top and sewing mitten seam.

THUMB

Round One: With the right side facing up, join COLOR A with a single crochet in the first of the eight skipped thumb stitches, single crochet in the next seven skipped thumb stitches then turn – eight single crochet.

Round Two: Chain one, single crochet in each single crochet across, turn. Repeat the last round until the thumb measure on one and a quarter inches, measured from round one of the thumb.

Round Three: Chain one (single crochet two stitches together) four times – four single crochets. Fasten off, leaving a long strand for gathering the top and sewing the thumb seam.

CORD (Make One)

With COLOR A, chain one hundred. Fasten off.

FINISHING

Using a yarn needle, thread the tail at the top of the thumb through the stitches of the final round and pull it gently in order to gather the material. With the loose strands, sew the sides of the thumb together. Then using the yarn needle, you should thread the tail at the top of the hand through the stitches of the final round and pull them gently to create a gather. Hold the tail, sew the sides of the mitten together, then sew each end of the cord to on mitten and connect the ends. Finally, sew the ribbon onto the top of each mitten.

Winter Baby Sack and Cap (Knit)

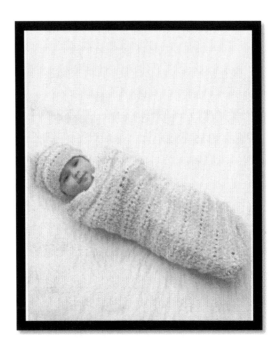

MEASUREMENTS:

Sack: Approximately 20" x 24" long.

Cap: One size to fit a newborn – three months.

MATERIALS:

- 4.5 mm Double Pointed Knitting Needle
- 4.5 mm Circular Knitting Needle
- One Color of Yarn (3 Balls)
- Marker

INSTRUCTIONS:

BACK

**Cast on eight stitches. Divide among three needles (two, three, three). Join in round, placing marker on the first stitch.

First and Alt Rounds: Knit

Second Round: * Increase by one in the next stitch. Repeat form * around. Sixteen stitches.

Fourth Round: * Knit one stitch. Increase by one in the next stitch. Repeat from * around. Twenty four stitches.

Sixth Round: * Knit two stitches. Increase by one in the next stitch. Repeat from * around. Thirty two stitches.

Eighth Round: * Knit three stitches. Increase by one in the next stitch. Repeat form * around. Forty stitches.

Tenth Round: * Knit four stitches. Increase by one in the next stitch. Repeat from * around. Forty eight stitches.

Twelfth Round: * Knit five stitches. Increase by one in the next stitch. Repeat from * around. Fifty six stitches **. Continue n the same manner, increase by eight stitches on the next and following alt round to ninety six stitches, changing to the circular needle when necessary.

*** Place the marker on the last round.   Working even in rounds, continue as follows:

First and Second Rounds: Purl.

Third Rounds: * Yarn over. Knit the next two stitches together. Repeat from * around.

Fourth and Fifth Rounds: Purl.

Sixth to Twelfth Rounds: Knit. ***

Repeat the last twelve rounds until the work from the marked round measures approximately twenty two inches, ending on a knit round.

Next Round: Purl.

Next Round: Knit. Repeat the last two rounds twice more. Cast off loosely.

CAP

Work from ** to ** same as the sack. Work from *** to *** same as the sack. Then repeat the last twelve rounds until the work from the marked round measures approximately four inches, ending on a knit round.

Next Round: Purl.

Next Round: Knit.   Repeat the last two rounds two more times.
Cast off loosely.

Winter Cozy Blanket (Knit)

MEASUREMENTS:

Approx 36" x 48" [91.5 x 122 cm]

MATERIALS:

- Knitting Needles (5 mm)
- Cable Needle
- One Color of Yarn (4 Balls)

INSTRUCTIONS:

Cast on seventy stitches. Do not join. Working back and forth in rows, continue as follows: Knit five (garter stitch), noting that the first row is wrong side, include eight stitches evenly across the last row. Seventy eight stitches.

Proceed in pattern as follows:

First Round (Right Side): Knit four stitches. Purl six stitches. (Wrok the first round of the cable panel pattern. Purl eight) twice. Work the first round of the cable panel pattern. Purl six stitches. Knit four stitches.

Second Round: Knit ten stitches. (Work the second row of the cable panel pattern. Knit eight stitches) twice. Work the second round of the cable panel pattern. Knit ten stitches.

Third Round: Knit four stitches. Purl six stitches. (Work the third row of the cable panel pattern. Purl eight) twice. Work the third row of the cable panel pattern. Purl six stitches. Knit four stitches.

Fourth Round: Knit ten stitches. (Work the fourth row of the cable panel pattern. Knit eight stitches) twice. Work the second round of the cable panel pattern. Knit ten stitches. Cable panel pattern is now in position. Continue cable panel pattern and proceed as established until the work from the beginning measures approximately forty six inches, ending on the twenty first row of the cable panel pattern.

Next Round (Wrong Side): Knit, decrease by eight stitches evenly across. Seventy stitches. Knit three rows (garter stitch). Cast off knitwise (Wrong Side).

Cable Panel Pattern (worked over fourteen stitches)

First Round (Right Side): Knit five stitches. Purl four stitches. Knit five stitches.

Second Round: Purl five stitches. Knit four stitches. Purl five stitches.

Third to Sixth Rounds: Repeat the first and second rounds two more times.

Seventh Round: Slip three stitches purlwise to a cable needle, and hold to the front of the work. Purl three stitches from the left needle. Knit three stitches from the cable needle. Purl two stitches. Slip three stitches purlwise to a cable needle, and hold to the back of the work. Knit three stitches from the left needle. Purl three stitches from the cable needle.

Eighth Round: Knit one stitch. Purl five stitches. Knit two stitches. Purl five stitches. Knit one stitch.

Ninth Round: Purl one stitch. Slip three stitches purlwise to a cable needle, and hold to the front of the work. Purl three stitches from the left needle. Knit three stitches from the cable needle. Slip three stitches purlwise to a cable needle, and hold to the back of the work. Knit three stitches from the left needle. Purl three stitches from the cable needle. Purl one stitch.

Tenth Round: Knit two stitches. Purl ten stitches. Knit two stitches.

Eleventh Round: Purl two stitches. Cable ten in front – Do this by holding the first five stitches on the cable needle and holding it in front of the work, knit five stitches on the left needle, then knit five stitches from the cable needle. Purl two stitches.

Twelfth Round: Repeat the tenth round.

Thirteenth Round: Purl one stitch. Slip three stitches purlwise to a cable needle, and hold to the back of the work. Knit three stitches from the left needle. Purl three stitches from the cable needle. Slip three stitches purlwise to a cable needle, and hold to the front of the work. Purl three stitches from the left needle. Knit three stitches from the cable needle. Purl one stitch.

Fourteenth Round: Repeat the eighth round.

Fifteenth Round: Slip three stitches purlwise to a cable needle, and hold to the back of the work. Knit three stitches from the left needle. Purl three stitches from the cable needle. Purl two stitches. Slip three stitches purlwise to a cable needle, and hold to the front of the work. Purl three stitches from the left needle. Knit three stitches from the cable needle.

Sixteenth Round: Repeat the second round.

Seventeenth to Twenty Eighth Rounds: Repeat the first and second rounds six more times.

These twenty eight rounds form the cable panel pattern.

Winter Slippers (Knit)

MEASUREMENTS:

To Fit Lady's shoe size 5/6 (7/8-9/10).

Finished Foot length

Small 5/6 9" [23 cm]

Medium 7/8 91/2" [24 cm]

Large 9/10 101/2" [26.5 cm]

MATERIALS:

- Knitting Needles (5.5 mm)
- One Ball of Yarn
- Fuzzy Cover
- Thread and Needle
- Scissors

- Three Markers

INSTRUCTIONS:

These instructions are written for the smallest size. If there are changes that need to be made for the larger sizes, the instructions will be written in the ( ).

Beginning at the back, using two strand of the MAIN COLOR, cast on two stitches.

First Round (Right Side): Knit.

Second Round: Increase one stitch by knitting into the front and back of the next stitch. Knit.

Third and Fourth Rounds: Knit.

Fifth Round: Increase one stitch by knitting into the front and back of the first stitch. Knit to the end of the round. Repeat the third to fifth rounds four more times. Eight stitches.

Next Two Round: Cast on ten stitches. Knit to the end of the round. Twenty eight stitches after the second round. Place marker on the last stitch of the last round. Work in garter stitch (knit every row) until the work from the marked row measures 41/2" [11.5 cm]. Then place a second set of markers at each end of the last row.

Knit for a further 3 (31/2-4)" [7.5 (9-10) cm] from the second set of markers and end with a wrong side round.

Shape Toe

First Round: Knit three stitches. *Knit the next two stitches together. Knit three stitches. Then repeat from * to the end of the round. Twenty three stitches.

Second Round: Knit.

Third Round: Knit three stitches. * Knit the next two stitches together. Knit two stitches. Next, repeat from * to the end of the round. Eighteen stitches.

Fourth Round: Knit.

Fifth Round: * Knit the next two stitches together. Knit one stitch. Next, repeat from * to the end of the round. Twelve stitches.

Sixth Round: (Knit the next two stitches together) six times. Six stitches. Break the yarn and leave a long end. Thread the end through the remaining stitches and draw up firmly. Fasten securely. Using a flat seam, sew the instep to a second set of markers. Sew the edges of the back triangle to cast on stitches of the sides to form the heel.

Fuzzy Cover

Beginning at the toe, using COLOR A, cast on ten stitches.

First Round (Wrong Side): Increase one stitch by knitting into the front and back of the next stitch. Knit to the end of the round.

Second Round: Increase one stitch by knitting into the front and back of the next stitch. Purl to the end of the row.

Repeat the last two rows three more times. Eighteen stitches. Place Marker at the end of the last row.

Beginning with a knit row, continue in reverse stocking stitch until the work from the marked row measures 3 (31/2-4)" [7.5 (9-10) cm], ending on a knit row. Next, place the marker at each end of the last row.

Divide for Sides

First Round (Right Side): Purl nine stitches. Turn. Leave the remaining stitches unworked. Continue on these nine stitches, work in reverse stocking stitch until the work from the last marker measures 41/2" [11.5 cm], ending on a knit row. Cast off.

With the wrong side facing up, join COLOR A to the remaining nine stitches. Continue on these nine stitches, work in the reverse stocking stitch until the work from the last marker measures 41/2" [11.5 cm], ending on a knit row. Cast off.

Sew cast off edges for back seam. Place the fuzzy cover on the top of the slipper. Using a thread and needle, sew it to the slipper around the foot opening. Stretch the fuzzy cover slightly over the slipper and sew in position around the bottom side edge.

Winter Fringed Scarf (Crochet)

MATERIALS:

- Crochet Hook (8mm)
- Yarn (4 Balls)
- Scissors
- Thread and Needle

INSTRUCTIONS:

Chain twenty six.

First Round (Right Side): One single crochet in the second chain from the hook. *Chain one. Miss the next chain. Do one single crochet in the next chain. Now, repeat from * to the end of the chain. Turn. Twenty five stitches.

Second Round: Chain one. Do one single crochet in the first single crochet. * One single crochet in the next one space chain. Chain one. Miss the next single crochet. Repeat from * to the last two stitches. Continue on to do another one single crochet in the next one space chain. Then do another one single crochet in the last single crochet. Turn.

Third Round: Chain one. Do one single crochet in the first single crochet. *Chain one. Skip the next single crochet. Then do one single crochet in the next one space chain. Repeat from * to the last two single crochet. Chain one. Miss the next single crochet. Continue on to do another single crochet in the last single crochet. Turn. Repeat the last two rows until the work from the beginning measures sixty six inches, ending on a wrong side row. Fasten off.

Fringe

Cut fourteen inches worth of yarn and take two strand of each color together, knot into the fringe evenly across the top and the bottom of the scarf. Cut the fringe evenly.

Manufactured by Amazon.ca
Bolton, ON

30262477R00031